WINNING IS A HABIT

VINCE LOMBARDI
ON WINNING,
SUCCESS, AND
THE PURSUIT OF
EXCELLENCE

EDITED BY
GARY R. GEORGE

HarperCollins*Publishers*

HarperCollins books may be purchased for educational, business, or sales promotional use. For information, please write to: Special Markets Department, HarperCollins Publishers, Inc., 10 East 53rd Street, New York, New York 10022.

FIRST EDITION

Designed by Joseph Rutt

Library of Congress Cataloging-in-Publication Data
Lombardi, Vince.
    Winning is a habit : Vince Lombardi on winning, success, and the pursuit of excellence / [edited by] Gary R. George. — 1st ed.
      p.   cm.
   ISBN 0–06–270215–7
   1. Lombardi, Vince—Quotations. 2. Football coaches—United States—Quotations. 3. Football—United States—Quotations, maxims, etc.   I. George, Gary R., 1954– . II. Title.
GV959.L75 1997   97–16121
796.332—dc21   CIP

---

99 00 01 ❖/HC 10 9 8 7 6 5 4 3

A portion of the proceeds from the sale of this book will be donated to the Vince Lombardi Cancer Clinic at St. Luke's Cancer Clinic in Milwaukee, Wisconsin, Special Olympics, and the Rawhide Boys Ranch. Contributions to the Vince Lombardi Cancer Clinic may be made by calling 1–800–252–2990, the Vince Lombardi Cancer Hotline.

Special thanks to Vince Lombardi, Jr., and the Estate of Vince Lombardi for their help and cooperation with this book.

Photographs courtesy of Vernon J. Biever.

To the memory of Horace R. George, a man who recognized great excellence in Vince Lombardi and his Green Bay Packers and a fan who made his son a part of that excellence. This book is dedicated to his life. In the end, Horace Raymond George was what he made of himself: a soldier and a lawyer, a husband and a father, a gentleman and a scholar, who was dedicated to his family, his country, his profession, his community, and his church. His life is a model to live by.

FOREWORD

Coach Vince Lombardi was the most effective coach I have ever known in preparing and motivating a team to win. In one of his great speeches, he asserted that how we practiced and played the game of pro football today was an example of how we would live the rest of our lives—if you continue to fail now, you will fail in your other careers after football. Because in the process of failure, we develop bad habits, and a habit, good or bad, soon becomes the natural thing to do. Successful people usually possess good habits.

Discipline and personal commitment were very

high in every aspect of Coach Lombardi's approach to getting things done. A statement made in one pre-game speech reminds me of life's daily challenges; he said "the quality of any man's life has got to be a full measure of that man's personal commitment to excellence and to victory regardless of what field he may be in."

"Winning is the only thing" became a controversy for many people who felt that there was too much emphasis on winning at all cost. However, Coach Lombardi reminded us many times that there is no laughter in losing.

Willie Davis

FOREWORD

In sports, as in business and life, every champion knows there are fundamentally strong building blocks necessary for victory and success. None is more profound than TEAMWORK.

Few men ever taught this lesson with the intensity and power of the legendary Vince Lombardi. A great teacher and leader, he was uniquely inspirational.

Never remotely interested in being good, he sought to excel and demanded that unselfish commitment from everyone in the interest of TEAM.

In this book, Lombardi's words display the power

of one of his messages: If you relentlessly chase per-
fection, you will enhance your God-given talents and
achieve excellence.

Bart Starr

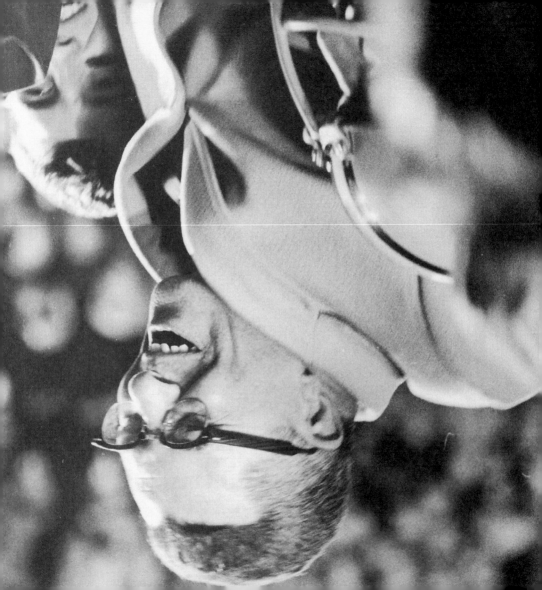

WINNING IS A HABIT

INTRODUCTION

Why is Vince Lombardi so special?

Vince Lombardi's life is a familiar story in the American Dream. Coach Lombardi grew up in an Italian family in New York. His hard work in school and his dedication to athletics led him to Fordham University and, eventually, into high school, college, and professional coaching. As a professional coach, he excelled as an assistant with the New York Giants and finally as head coach and general manager of the Green Bay Packers during the 1960s. This was a time when professional football was bursting onto the nation's conscience because of television. Coach Lombardi's victories in the "Ice Bowl" of 1967 against the Dallas Cowboys and in Super Bowls I and II created a special place for him in the annals of the National Football League and the history of professional sports.

It is his philosophy and his words of inspiration—whether to sporting teams or business groups—that have made him a standard by which other coaches and motivational speakers are judged.

This book is intended to identify some of those words and speeches in a way that reveals the ongoing usefulness of Coach Lombardi's wisdom. His views on family, religion, loyalty, and perseverance are as important to all citizens as his specific words on football are to coaches and fans.

The continuing power of Coach Lombardi's words and success so long after his passing remains a part of his many legacies. It can be seen in the lives of those players he touched who have gone on to tremendous success, such as Willie Davis, Bart Starr, and Frank Gifford. It can be seen in the work of the Vince Lombardi Cancer Clinic in Milwaukee, Wisconsin, at Saint Luke's Hospital, as well as in the frequent uses of his image for marketing in the 1990s. Coach Lombardi inspires us. Coach Lombardi inspires me.

In 1967, Willie Davis and my father, Attorney Horace R. George, were friends based on their relationship to Grambling University in Louisiana. That year, Willie Davis generously gave my father and me—

a Milwaukee seventh grader at the time—the opportunity to go to the "Ice Bowl," where the Packers played the Cowboys for the NFL Championship. During one of the coldest sporting events ever, when the wind chill was well below zero, Bart Starr called a quarterback sneak to score a touchdown and win the game. This brought about a finer focus on the clear association between Coach Lombardi and his Packers and the concepts of winning and excellence. I and many other people of my generation grew up with that image; we have been motivated by it and have tried to teach it to our children.

It is my hope that this book allows those who have directly experienced the excellence and wisdom of Coach Lombardi to re-experience it. It is also my hope that those who have never known the greatness of the man who spoke the words "Winning isn't everything, it's the only thing" will find motivation to pursue excellence and to persevere in that pursuit, whether it's on the football field, in the classroom, in the workplace, or in any other of life's everyday activities.

Gary R. George
Milwaukee, Wisconsin
July 1997

WINNING

Winning isn't everything. It's the only thing.

■

Winning is not a sometime thing; it's an all-the-time thing. You don't win once in a while, you don't do things right once in a while, you do them right all the time. Winning is a habit. Unfortunately, so is losing. . . .

It's a reality of life that men are competitive and the most competitive games draw the most competitive men. That's why they're there—to compete. They know the rules and the objectives when they get in the game. The objective is to win—fairly, squarely, decently, by the rules—but to win.

The will to excel and the will to win, they endure. They are more important than any events that occasion them. I don't care what people say about me as long as I win. That's what I get paid for.

There is no room for second place here. There is one place here and that's first place. I've finished second twice in my time here, and I don't ever want to finish second again. There's a second place bowl game, and it's a hinky-dinky football game, held in a hinky-dinky town, played by hinky-dinky football players. That's all second place is: Hinky-Dinky.

It isn't good enough to say we're rebuilding.
I am sick of people who apologize for a bad job.

■

*After the 33–14 Green Bay victory over
Oakland in Super Bowl II, January 14, 1968:*
This is the best way to leave a football field.

Before the December 31, 1967, game where it was −13 degrees:

You've got to be bigger than the weather to be a winner.

■

Explaining why he has to be harsh with his players:

My job is winning championships for the Green Bay Packers. That comes first. . . the Packers and winning championships. . . before everything else. . . the press, television, radio, my fff—no, not my family, but everything else.

You don't have to win 'em aesthetically. You win 'em the best you can.

■

I don't give a damn about statistics as long as we win.

Anybody can lose, and I'm not here to teach you how to be a good loser. Anybody can be a good loser. I'm teaching you how to be a good winner. There is no substitute for winning. You have to be a bad loser—a hard loser.

Winning is like a drug. It's a hard thing to kick.

—

The zeal to be first in everything has always been American, to win, to win, and to win.

It's easy to have faith in yourself and have discipline when you're a winner, when you're number one. What you got to have is faith and discipline when you're not yet a winner.

All of the glamour, all of the noise, all of the excitement, all of the color, they linger only in the memory, but the spirit, the will to excel, the will to win, they go on forever.

Second place is meaningless. You can't always be first, but you have to believe that you should have been—that you are never beaten, time just runs out on you.

■

Before a season-opener:
I'm here because we win. You're here because we win. When we lose, we're gone.

There are only five or six big plays in every game and you have to make them to win. In a time of crisis, it is absolutely imperative.

■

If you don't think you're a winner, you don't belong here.

The trouble with me is that my ego just can't accept a loss. I suppose that if I were more perfectly adjusted I could toss off defeat, but my name is on this ball club. Thirty-six men publicly reflect me and reflect on me, and it's a matter of my pride.

Regarding his infamous saying "Winning isn't everything, it's the only thing":

I wish to hell I'd never said the damned thing. I meant the effort. . . I meant having a goal. . . . I sure as hell didn't mean for people to crush human values and morality.

THE
GREEN BAY
PACKERS

After the 21–17 victory over Dallas in the December 31, 1967, game:

We went for a touchdown instead of a field goal because I didn't want all those freezing people up in the stands to have to sit through a sudden death.

—

We are the World Champion Green Bay Packers, and everyone who wears a Green Bay Packers uniform should act like a world champion, on the field and off.

Talking to his team early in the season:
Your whole life is ahead of you. Most of my life
is behind me.

My life now is the Green Bay Packers.

To the press in 1958 about his prospective future in Green Bay:

After all, I need to win only two games next season and Green Bay will have improved 100 percent.

When stranded by a snowstorm in Green Bay in 1950 while recruiting for West Point:

Can you imagine anybody living in a place like this? This is just the end of the world.

■

Said often to his players:

You were chosen to be a Green Bay Packer.

When asked if his players (in Washington) were afraid they'd lose their jobs:

I suppose there are certain players afraid of their future. The Packers over the course of time came to see that my wrath was not as dangerous as it sounded.

■

There are three things that are important to every man in this room. His religion, his family, and the Green Bay Packers, in that order.

I'm going to tell you the facts, gentlemen, and the facts are these: At Green Bay, we have winners. We do not have losers. If you're a loser, mister, you're going to get your ass out of here and you're going to get your ass out of here right now. Gentlemen, we are paid to win. Gentlemen, we will win.

SUCCESS
AND THE
PURSUIT OF
EXCELLENCE

If you quit now, during these workouts, you'll quit in the middle of the season in a game. Once you learn to quit it becomes a habit. We don't want anyone here who'll quit. We want 100 percent out of every individual, and if you don't want to give it, get out. Just get up and get out right now.

Fatigue makes a coward of us all. When you're tired you rationalize. You make excuses in your mind. You say, "I'm too tired, I'm bushed, I can't do this, I'll loaf." Then you're a coward.

■

Defining the "willingness to suffer":
It means you got home a little later, a little wearier, a little hungrier, and with a few more aches and pains.

Truly, I have never known a really successful man who deep in his heart did not understand the grind, the discipline it takes to win.

But to achieve success, whatever the job we have, we must pay a price for success. It's like anything worthwhile. It has a price.

■

Confidence is contagious. So is lack of confidence.

If you really want something, you can have it if you are willing to pay the price. And the price means that you have to work better and harder than the next guy.

■

Leaders are made, they are not born; and they are made just like anything else has been made in this country—by hard effort. And that's the price that we all have to pay to achieve that goal, or any goal.

If you could have won, you should have.

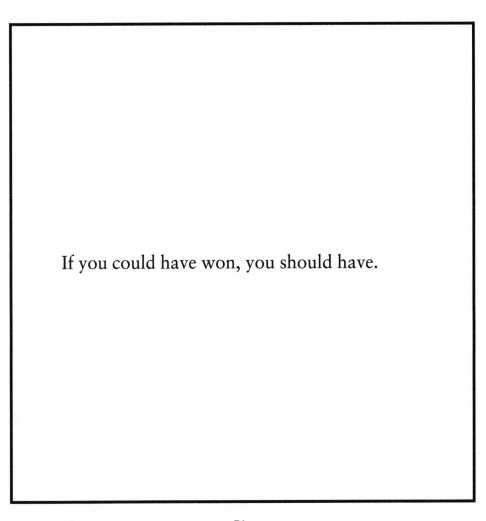

I've never known a man worth his salt who in the long run, deep down in his heart, didn't appreciate the grind, the discipline. There is something in good men that really yearns for, needs, discipline and the harsh reality of head-to-head combat.

The harder you work, the harder it is to surrender.

■

The closer you get to the goal line, the more crucial the situation, the more perfect you should be. . . .

There is no substitute for work.

■

Competition builds stamina in an individual, character, aggressiveness, and there is no more competitive game than football.

The real glory is being knocked to your knees and then coming back.

■

How does a man meet his failures? That is the measure of the man. If he does not quit or curl up he has the right stuff in him. Be a hard loser.

Physical toughness will make the opponent weaken and mental toughness will make him crack.

■

No one is perfect, but boys, making the effort to be perfect. . . is what life is all about. . . . If you'll not settle for anything less than the best, you will be amazed at what you can do with your lives.

The greatest accomplishment is not in never falling, but in rising again after you fall.

■

What I criticize people for is mental errors, not physical ones.

The quality of any man's life has got to be a full measure of that man's personal commitment to excellence and victory, regardless of what field he may be in.

■

We. . . shall play every game to the hilt with every ounce of fiber we have in our bodies.

We want to perfect ourselves so that we can win with less struggle and increasing ease, but the strange thing is that it's not the easy wins we ostensibly seek but rather the difficult struggles to which we look forward.

◼

You don't do things right once in a while. You do them right all the time.

Hurt is in the mind.

■

It is the same every week. You spend six days building for one opponent, and on Monday you have to forget it. Win or lose, if you don't put it behind you, you'll be wading around all week knee-deep in confusion.

What I want you to do is to start to get yourself into shape mentally. I want you to ache to get back into action. I want you to be aggressive. I want aggressive players. I want players who are aggressive even when it hurts.

■

A team that thinks it's going to lose is going to lose.

Not everyone can be a winner all the time, but everyone can make that effort, that commitment to excellence.

■

Teams do not go physically flat, but they go mentally stale.

On mental toughness:

I think it's singleness of purpose and, once you have agreed upon the price that you and your family must pay for success, it enables you to forget that price. It enables you to ignore the minor hurts, the opponent's pressure, and the temporary failures.

Football teaches mental toughness. That's the most important phase of the game to me. Mental toughness is humility. Mental toughness is a disciplined will above anything else. What I mean by that is that disciplined will is your own character in action.

■

The only true satisfaction a player receives is the satisfaction that comes from being part of a successful team.

You defeat defeatism with confidence.

ON
FAITH
IN GOD

At a testimonial dinner in Green Bay in 1962:
[I want to thank] the good Lord for His help
and His understanding. And I pray to Him each
day to give me enough sense of humor to be serious
but never allow me to take myself too seriously.

■

Never pray for victory, pray for the will of God.

We don't pray to win. We pray to play the best we can and to keep us free from injury. And the prayer we say after the game is one of thanksgiving.

■

After diagnosed with colon cancer and hospitalized for surgery and treatment:

I'm not afraid to meet my God now. But what I do regret is that there is so damn much left to be done on earth.

I don't say these things because I believe in the "brute" nature of man or that men must be brutalized to be combative. I believe in God, and I believe in human decency. But I firmly believe that any man's finest hour—his greatest fulfillment to all he holds dear—is that moment when he has worked his heart out in a good cause and lies exhausted on the field of battle—victorious.

You seldom, if ever, find an athlete who is a criminal. He is essentially a good boy, a good sport, and a gentleman. He adheres to the word of God, call it the Golden Rule if you will, both on the field and off. . . . I am going to raise my son to be an athlete.

SPEECHES
TO
BUSINESS
LEADERS

When asked how to achieve discipline:

You have to sell yourself to them, to the group. And in order to sell yourself to the group, there is no way you can be dishonest about it. Therefore, what you sell has to come from the heart, and it has to be something you really believe in. That belief can be anything. It can be just the plain belief in the game of football, right?

Speech to a business group in Dayton, Ohio:

I have picked up a reputation for being tough or for being hard. . . and I admit I have some mixed emotions about that reputation, particularly when one of my former players was asked, "What is it like to work with Vince Lombardi?" and his answer was, "Well, I'll tell you in a nutshell. When Lombardi turns to us in the locker room and tells us to sit down, I don't even look for a chair."

Speech to the American Management Association in New York, February 8, 1967:

[Football] is a symbol of what this country's best attributes are—namely, courage, stamina, and coordinated efficiency. It is a spartan game, and I mean by that, it requires spartanlike qualities in order to play it and I am speaking of the spartan qualities of sacrifice and self-denial rather than that other spartan quality of leaving the weak to die. It's a game very much like life in that it demands that a man's personal commitment must be to an excellence and victory, and yet complete victory can never be completely won. Yet it must be pursued, it must be wooed with all of one's might.

In a large sense, we are engaged right now in a struggle that is far more fiercely contested than any game. It is a struggle for the hearts, for the minds, and for the souls of all of us, and it is a game in which there are no spectators, only players, and it is a struggle which will test all of our courage, all of our stamina, and all of our leadership ability, and only if we are physically, mentally, and spiritually ready will we win this one.

We live in an age for heroes. No other time in our history has ever offered the prizes and the perils at one and the same time so great. Man must decide whether he wants to provide a full life for humanity or destroy himself with his own problems. The test of this century will be whether man mistakes the growth of wealth and power with the growth of spirit and character or, like some infant playing with dangerous toys, he destroys the very house he may have inherited. . . . I think we fail miserably in our obligation unless we preserve what has always been an American zeal and that is to be first in regardless what we do and to win and to win and to win.

The prevailing sentiment seems to be if you don't like the rule, break it. . . . Everything has been done to strengthen the rights of the individual and at the same time, weaken the rights of the church, weaken the rights of the state, and weaken the rights of all authority. . . . Maybe we have too much freedom.

The leader must be willing to use it. His leadership is then based on truth and character. There must be truth in the purpose and willpower in the character. Leadership rests not only upon ability, but upon commitment and upon loyalty and upon pride and upon followers.

A leader is composed of not just one quality, but a blend of many, and each must develop their own particular combination to their own personality.

■

In spite of what many think, none of us are really born equal, and the talented have no more responsibility for their birthright than the underprivileged for theirs. The measure of each is what each does in a specific situation.

It is increasingly difficult to be tolerant of a society which seems to have sympathy only for the misfits, only for the maladjusted, only for the criminal, only for the loser. Have sympathy for them, yes; help them, yes; but I think it is also time for us to cheer for, to stand up for, to stand behind the doer, the achiever, the one who recognizes a problem and does something about it, the one who looks for something to do for his country; the winner, the leader.

Mental toughness is spartanism with its qualities of sacrifice and self-denial, dedication, fearlessness, and love. The love I'm speaking of is not necessarily liking or the love that a man may have for his wife. The love I'm speaking of is loyalty, which is the greatest of loves. Teamwork, the love that one man has for another and that he respects the dignity of another. The love I am speaking of is charity.

You show me a man who belittles another and I will show you a man who is not a leader; or one who is not charitable, who has no respect for the dignity of another, is not loyal, and I will show you a man who is not a leader.

I am not advocating that love which forces everyone to love the white man because he is white or the black man because he is black or the poor because he is poor or your enemy because he is your enemy, but rather of a love that one man has for another human being, any human being who happens to be white or black, rich or poor, enemy or friend. . . . Heart power is the strength of America, and hate power is the weakness of the world.

Mental toughness is also the perfectly disciplined will. The strength of the group is in the will of the leader, and the will is the character in action. The great hope of society is the character in action. We are never going to create a good society, much less a great one, until individual excellence is once more respected and encouraged.

■

If we will create something, we must be something.

No leader, however great, can long continue unless he wins battles. The battle decides all. How does one achieve success in battle? I believe it is essential to understand that battles are won primarily in the hearts of men. Men respond to leadership in a most remarkable way, and once you have won his heart, he will follow you anywhere.

Leadership is based on a spiritual quality, the power to inspire, the power to inspire others to follow. This spiritual quality may be for good or for evil. In many cases in the past, this quality has been devoted toward personal ends and was partly or wholly evil. Leadership which is evil, while it may temporarily succeed, always carries within itself the seeds of its own destruction.

The obvious difference between the group and the man who leads them is not in lack of strength, not in lack of knowledge, but rather in lack of will. The character, rather than education, is man's greatest need and man's greatest safeguard because character is higher than intellect. While it is true the difference between men is in energy, in the strong will, in the settled purpose, and in the invincible determination, the new leadership is in sacrifice, it is in self-denial, it is in love and loyalty, it is in fearlessness, it is in humility, and it is in the perfectly disciplined will. This, gentlemen, is the distinction between great and little men.

THE
PLAYERS

To the rookies:

Some of you boys are having problems picking up your assignments. It's a tough task. You got so many plays to learn, so many moves to learn. If you make a mistake, if you drop a pass or miss a block, anything like that, hell, forget it. If we had a defensive back here who felt bad every time he got beat on a pass pattern, he wouldn't be worth a damn. Take an education, but don't dwell on it. Don't let it affect your play. You will drop passes. You will make mistakes. But not very many if you want to play for the Green Bay Packers.

To Larry Brown:

Larry, you're a hell of an athlete. You can get mad at me, you can call me anything you want to call me, but don't say it when I'm around because then you're challenging me, and I'm the head coach.

After catching Max McGee sneaking out for the third time:

Max, I said that will cost you five hundred dollars and if you go again, it'll cost you a thousand. Max, if you can find anything worth sneaking out for a thousand dollars, hell, call me and I'll go with you.

To Paul Hornung before the 1959 season:

I know your reputation here. I've investigated you very carefully. You have done things you shouldn't have done. . . . I trust you. I just don't want you to let me down. If you do, it'll be your [ass].

To Paul Hornung:

You're my halfback. The only way you can get out of the job is to get killed.

[Bart] Starr has more command of a game than any man I know. He makes me look like the greatest coach in the business.

When asked how much help he gave Starr during a game:

We go to school during the week. By game time, we've got every situation covered. The only time I say anything is if [Starr] forgets, but Bart doesn't forget.

To Lee Roy Caffey:

Lee Roy, if you cheat on the practice field, you'll cheat in the game. If you cheat in the game, you'll cheat the rest of your life. I'll not have it. . . . Lee Roy, you may think I criticize you too much, a little unduly at times. You have the size, the strength, the speed, the mobility, everything in the world necessary to be a great football player, except one thing. YOU'RE TOO DAMN LAZY.

To Jerry Kramer:

Kramer! The concentration period of a college student is thirty minutes, maybe less. Of a high-school student, fifteen minutes, maybe less. In junior high, it's about five minutes, and in kindergarten, it's about one minute. You can't remember anything for even one minute! Where in the hell does that put you?

Game-day pep talk:

You owe something to these people who are coming out to see you today. When this game ends, I want them to say they just saw the greatest team they ever saw. They just saw the greatest defensive end they ever saw. They just saw the greatest offensive guard they ever saw. If they don't come out saying that, your record doesn't mean anything.

At a labor negotiation meeting when a speaker demeaned the players:

Good God, man! Don't you realize that these men are artists? You aren't dealing with a bunch of hod carriers or truck drivers. These men are artists, skilled artists, dammit!

■

Regarding excessive contract demands by players, especially those who issue ultimatums:

They both get hustled out of my office in a hurry, and the one with the ultimatum, if he does not relent, gets traded.

On the evening of July 23, 1959, before the first practice, Vince explained his approach to squeamish veterans in a dynamic, uncompromising speech:

Gentlemen, we're going to have a football team. We are going to win some games. Do you know why? Because you are going to have confidence in me and my system. By being alert you are going to make fewer mistakes than your opponents. By working harder you are going to outexecute, outblock, outtackle every team that comes your way. I've never been a losing coach, and I don't intend to start here. There is nobody big enough to think he's got the team made or can do what he wants. Trains and planes are going in and coming out of Green Bay every day, and he'll be on one of them. I won't. I'm going to find thirty-six men who have the pride to make any sacrifice to win. There are such men. If they're not here, I'll get them. If you are not one, if you don't want to play, you might as well leave right now. . . . I've been up here all year and I've learned a lot. I know how the townspeople are and what they think of you men and I know that in a small town you need definite rules and regulations. And anybody who breaks the rules will be taken care of in my own way. . . . You may not be a tackle. You may not be a back. But you *will* be a professional.

THE
WRATH OF
LOMBARDI

A man who's late for meetings or the bus won't run his pass routes right. He'll be sloppy.

■

After a bad practice:
If you don't do better tomorrow, then you're not going to get Sunday off. Nothing says you have to have a day off. I give a day off and if you don't perform you don't get a day off.

There's no place on this team, or in this nation, for a loser! I get paid to win! We're going to win! I take pride in winning. So do you.

■

After losing a championship game in Philadelphia:

Perhaps you didn't realize that you could have won this game. We are men and we will never let this happen again. Now we can start preparing for next year.

The year following the second consecutive loss of the Western Division title, Lombardi kicked off the season by saying:

You're still a first-place team. You just quit paying the price, that's all. This season, you're going to pay.

After the first scrimmage in 1967:

Some of you people are fat. You're fat in the head, fat in the body. You're out of shape. It's an absolute disgrace the way you came into camp. That twenty-five thousand dollars you all made at the end of last year for winning the Super Bowl made you all fatheaded. You're lazy.

During Giants training camp:
You are without a doubt the dumbest bunch of supposed college graduates I've ever had the misfortune to be associated with in my life.

—

What kind of an excuse for a block is that?

You fellows are supposed to be a championship team, but you must have been lucky to get where you are. Let's get back at it and do it right.

■

Don't think you're responsible for all this success. Don't let it go to your heads and become impressed with yourselves, because I want you to understand that *I* did this. *I* made you guys what you are.

Goddamnit, you guys don't care if you win or lose. I'm the only one that cares. I'm the only one that puts his blood and his guts and his heart into the game! You guys show up, you listen a little bit. . . . You've got the concentration of three-year-olds. You're nothing! I'm the only guy that gives a damn if we win or lose.

■

You're standing around here with your fingers up your nose.

Nobody wants to pay the price. I'm the only one here that's willing to pay the price. You guys don't care. You don't want to win.

■

To get himself in a bad mood in order to "chew out" the players:

I'll get up early in the morning and have a fight with Marie. Then I'll really bury that ball club. I'll be ready to yell all day.

If you give me anything less than your best, you're not only cheating yourself, your coaches, your teammates, everybody in Green Bay and everything pro football stands for. You're also cheating the Maker who gave you that talent. I know we don't have cheaters on this ball club.

■

I don't want to seem ungrateful, I'm awfully proud of you guys, really. You've done a hell of a job. But sometimes you just disgust me.

When I say "hate," I don't mean I wish anybody any physical harm. Do I mean I want to run out on the field and hit a man, or kick him, or fall on top of him and pummel him? No. I wouldn't do that. But I do have to build up an emotion before a game to do a good job. If I go out there feeling just fine about everything and everybody, I'm not going to do the job I should do.

Justifying his abusiveness:

Hell, I can't just sit around and see an error being made and not say anything about it. I like to think I've had some experience in this business, and you don't win when you're making a lot of errors. Nobody wants to be told they're making errors, not the way I tell them. But they got to be told and told until they get to the point where they don't make them anymore.

I don't like to single out people. You always forget some you shouldn't when you do.

When asked if he liked to think of himself as a heartless man:

No. Why would anybody? It's no damn fun being hard. I've been doing this for years and years and years. It's never been great fun. You have to drive yourself constantly. I don't enjoy it. It takes a hell of a lot out of me. And, Christ, you get kind of embarrassed with yourself for doing it, for being in a job where you have to. Fortunately, I don't remember.

All I want to know is how far can I push a guy.

■

This is a game of inches. I don't ever want to see you stopped by inches again. If you get this close and you don't make it, I'm going to come out and kick your butt.

THE
ART OF
COACHING

To his assistant coaches regarding professionalism:

Gentlemen, we are coming downtown every day into the heart of the business district, among professional people in their shirts and ties. It would be a sorry thing if we came in with a bunch of cowboy clothes.

To his assistant coaches:

I demand the best from all of you. I'm a perfectionist, and there's absolutely no excuse for anything other than that.

■

The difference between teaching and coaching is selling yourself, being involved right up to your neck. . . . And to be a teacher, you got to win their hearts. Once you win a team's heart they'll follow you anywhere, they'll do anything for you.

You've got to win the hearts of the people that you lead. The personality of the individual has to do it—the incandescence. . . . There's no hereditary strata in leading. They're not born; they're made. There has to be an inclination, a commitment, a willingness to command.

The most important thing a coach needs is the knowledge that his team can or can't play under pressure. If it can't you need new players; if it can, you can make do with average ones.

■

In all my years of coaching, I have never been successful using somebody else's play.

I hold it more important to have the players' confidence than their affection.

■

When asked to postpone or cancel practice that coincided with the scheduled deadline of the Cuban Missile Crisis:

The hell with Cuba. Let's get to work.

Hell, I'm an emotional man. I cry. . . . I'm not ashamed of crying. Football's an emotional game. You can't be a cold fish and go out and coach. If you're going to be involved in it, you gotta take your emotions with you.

■

They call it coaching, but it is teaching. You do not just tell them. . . you show them the reasons.

You fit your game to the talents and personality of your team as well as to your own.

■

In coaching you speak in clichés, but I mean every one of them.

To a reporter:

Are you trying to be funny? Are you trying to be a comedian? I don't like comedians. . . . This isn't a funny game.

▄

My game is pro football, not "Twenty Questions."

During retirement, he lamented:

There's a great—a great *closeness* on a football team, a rapport between the men and the coach that's like no other sport. It's a binding together, a knitting together. For me, it's like father and sons. . . . I missed players coming up to me and saying, "Coach, I need some help because my baby's sick," or, "Mr. Lombardi, I want to talk to you about trouble I'm having with my wife."

The strength of a group is in the strength of the leader. Many mornings when I am worried or depressed, I have to give myself what is almost a pep talk, because I am not going before that ball club without being able to exude assurance. I must be the first believer, because there is no way you can hoodwink the players.

THE
GAME OF
FOOTBALL

Football is a hard-headed, cold business. No matter what a player did last year, if he can't do it this year he has to go.

■

After the Giants' loss to the Colts in their first playoff:

I have only two complaints about [the season]. It was a couple of inches too short and seven seconds too long.

Dancing is a contact sport. Football is a collision sport.

■

Football is a way of life.

Some of our offensive linemen are too nice sometimes. This is a violent sport. That's why crowds love it, that's why people love it, because it's a violent sport, a body contact sport. We're a little too nice. We've got to be a little meaner.

Football is a game of abandon. You run with complete abandon. You care for nothing or anybody. I don't want a tank or a wall or a dozen men to stop you.

Description of one of the basic football skills:
If a man is running down the street with everything you own, you won't let him get away. That's tackling.

■

A few key plays decide each football game, and you never know when a key play is going to come up.

When Fordham dropped their football program in 1954:

A university without football is in danger of deteriorating into a medieval study hall.

■

Football is a game of many lessons in courage, stamina and teamwork. It's a spartan game and requires spartan qualities. Sacrifice, self-discipline, dedication—these are spartan qualities.

Football is a simple game. Television has most of the people believing it's something complicated. One of these days, if you don't watch out, the public won't be buying it.

RACISM

If you're black or white, you're a part of the family. We make no issue over a man's color. I just won't tolerate anybody in this organization, coach or player, making it an issue. We respect every man's dignity, black or white. I won't stand for any movements or groups on our ball club. It comes down to a question of love. . . . You just have to love your fellow man, and it doesn't matter whether he is black or white. If anything is bothering any of our players—black and white alike—we settle whatever it is right away.

After losing a confrontation with local authorities in Jacksonville, Florida, over segregated accommodations during the 1962 season, Vince tearfully told his black players:

I'll never—absolutely never—put you guys in this situation again. If it means we play no games down here, that's the way it will be.

■

About race relations on the Redskins:

I'm not saying I don't know who's black and who's white on the club. I'm just saying that I have no sense of it when I'm dealing with my people.

In response to the question "How many blacks do you have on your squad?":

I can tell you how many players I have on the squad and I can tell you which ones aren't going to be here next year. But I can't tell you how many are black and how many are white.

If I ever hear any man on this squad use the words "nigger," "dago" or other derogatory racial slur, you're through with this team. I won't stand for that.